Andrew Brodie

Improving
Comprehension

for ages 8–9

A & C Black • London

Contents

*Extract from *The Hodgeheg* by Dick King Smith. Reproduced by permission of Hamish Hamilton, 1987

** Extract from *Horrid Henry's Stinkbomb* by Francesca Simon. Reproduced by permission of Orion Books

*** Extract from *Stig of the dump* by Clive King. Reproduced by permission of Puffin, 1963

Introduction

Improving Comprehension includes a range of interesting and exciting texts for sharing with pupils and using for reading comprehension. The texts have been carefully selected to be appropriate to the age group and to cover a range of text types. They reflect the demands of the Primary Framework for Literacy and in particular they following the learning objectives for Year 4. The accompanying comprehension worksheets are differentiated at three levels and are designed to be used by individuals or small groups. *Notes for teachers* are provided at the bottom of each worksheet providing guidance on how to get the most from the texts and how to approach the questions on the sheet.

For monitoring and recording purposes an *Individual record sheet* is provided on page 4 detailing reading and writing levels appropriate for Year 4. You may also find it helpful to refer to the *Contents* page where the 'texts' are linked to the relevant Assessment Focuses.

How to use the book and CD-ROM together

The book has fifteen 'texts', which can be projected on to a whiteboard for whole class use using the CD-ROM, or photocopied/printed for use with small groups or individuals. Sharing the text either on screen or on paper provides lots of opportunities for speaking and listening, for decoding words through a phonic approach, for reading and re-reading for meaning and for satisfaction and enjoyment in shared success.

For each text there are three comprehension worksheets at different ability levels to enable teachers to differentiate across the ability range. An animal picture at the top of the sheet indicates the level of the worksheet. The 'cat' exercises are at the simplest level; the 'dog' exercises are at the next level; the 'rabbit' exercises are at the most advanced level. You may decide to give some pupils the 'cat' worksheet and then decide, on the basis of their success, to ask them to complete the 'dog' worksheet. A similar approach could be taken with the 'dog' and 'rabbit' sheets.

After reading the text with the pupils the teacher should discuss the tasks with the children, ensuring that they understand clearly how to complete the worksheet and reminding them to answer the questions using full sentences and correct punctuation.

National Curriculum levels

The worksheets are aimed at the following ability levels:

Cat worksheets are for pupils working confidently at Level 2.
Dog worksheets are for pupils working towards Level 3.
Rabbit worksheets are for pupils who are working confidently at Level 3.

Individual record sheet

Pupil's name: _____

Date of birth: _____

Reading Level 2

☐ I can show understanding when reading simple texts.
☐ My reading of simple texts is generally accurate.
☐ I can express opinions about major events or ideas in stories, poems and non-fiction.
☐ I can use phonic skills in reading unfamiliar words and establishing meaning.
☐ I can use graphic skills in reading unfamiliar words and establishing meaning.
☐ I can use syntactic skills in reading unfamiliar words and establishing meaning.
☐ I can use contextual skills in reading unfamiliar words and establishing meaning.

Reading Level 3

☐ I can read a range of texts fluently and accurately.
☐ I can read independently.
☐ I use strategies appropriately to establish meaning.
☐ In my responses to fiction I show understanding of the main points and I express preferences.
☐ In my responses to non-fiction I show understanding of the main points and I express preferences.
☐ I know the order of the alphabet.
☐ I use my knowledge of the alphabet to locate books and find information.

Writing Level 2

☐ My narrative writing communicates meaning.
☐ My non-narrative writing communicates meaning.
☐ I use appropriate and interesting vocabulary.
☐ I show some awareness of the reader.
☐ I can write a sequence of sentences to show ideas developing.
☐ My sentences are sometimes demarcated by capital letters and full stops.
☐ Usually, I can spell simple, monosyllabic words correctly or spell a phonetically plausible alternative.
☐ My letters are accurately formed.
☐ My letters are consistent in size.

Writing Level 3

☐ My writing is often organised, imaginative and clear.
☐ I use the main features of different forms of writing.
☐ I am beginning to adapt my writing to different readers.
☐ I use sequences of sentences to extend ideas logically.
☐ I choose words for variety and interest.
☐ The basic grammatical structure of my sentences is usually correct.
☐ My spelling is usually accurate, including that of common, polysyllabic words.
☐ I use punctuation accurately to mark sentences, including full stops, capital letters and question marks.
☐ My handwriting is joined and legible.

Sports Day

Tariq's legs were shaking. He was terrified. Everybody else was better than him. Yusuf could run really fast, Euan was brilliant at football, Satish was always charging around the playground and Sam was probably the fastest of them all.

"Ready boys?" asked Mrs Carson.

The boys nodded and grinned. Well, most of them grinned, apart from Tariq who was too frightened. They stepped up to the starting line and Mrs Carson held up the little flag. It was a Union Jack flag that she'd kept since Prince William had visited the town.

"Ready, … steady, … go!" called Mrs Carson as she dropped the flag quickly. But Tariq was already away, his feet pounding along the track.

"STOP!" shouted Mrs Carson.

Tariq kept running as fast as he could but looked round anxiously. Something was wrong. No-one else was running.

"STOP!" shouted Mrs Carson again. She looked angry. "Tariq, why didn't you stop when I asked you to?"

Tariq stopped running and headed back towards the starting line. The other boys were staring at him and laughing.

"Do you know why I stopped you?" asked Mrs Carson crossly.

Tariq shook his head.

"You set off before I said 'go'. That's typical of you Tariq. Were you trying to cheat?" said Mrs Carson, her eyes wide with anger.

"I don't know why he's racing anyway," said Sam, "he's going to lose because he's a loser." The other boys sniggered. Tariq felt as angry as Mrs Carson.

"Right, let's try again shall we?" said Mrs Carson.

The boys lined up again and Mrs Carson raised the flag. "Ready …" Tariq put one foot forward. "Steady …" Tariq clenched his fists. "Go!"

Tariq paused for a moment then shot forward. He hammered each foot against the ground and ran with huge strides, his anger feeding his energy. He ignored the other runners. He ignored the rest of the school and the parents who were watching, and most of all he ignored Mrs Carson.

Within seconds he burst across the finishing line, ran on for a few metres, then turned and watched as the other four boys crossed the line.

"Who's a loser now?" he asked Sam.

Andrew Brodie: Improving Comprehension for ages 8-9 © A&C Black Publishers Ltd 2008

Sports Day

Name: _____

Date: _____

Answer the questions, using full sentences. Check your punctuation carefully.

1. Why was Tariq frightened?

   _____

   _____

2. What did Mrs Carson hold up ready to start the race?

   _____

   _____

3. Why did Mrs Carson stop the race?

   _____

   _____

4. Which boy said something unkind about Tariq?

   _____

   _____

5. Who won the race?

   _____

   _____

6. Write about a race you have been in and how you felt.

   _____

   _____

   _____

   _____

   _____

Notes for teachers

Help the children to read the passage slowly and carefully, ensuring that they understand the story and how the different characters might be feeling. Discuss the questions with them and encourage them to work out their answers orally before putting anything down on paper. As an extension activity you could discuss the behaviour of the characters in this story. Did the boys behave well? Did Mrs Carson behave well? Did Tariq behave well?

Sports Day

Name: _____

Date: _____

Answer the questions, using full sentences.

1. How many boys were taking part in the race?

   _____

   _____

2. Why didn't Tariq grin when Mrs Carson asked the boys if they were ready?

   _____

   _____

3. Why was Mrs Carson angry?

   _____

   _____

4. Why was Tariq angry?

   _____

   _____

5. Describe how Tariq ran in the race.

   _____

   _____

6. On a separate sheet of paper, write about a race that you have taken part in or a race that you have watched.

Notes for teachers
Help the children to read this passage slowly and carefully, discussing the feelings of the characters involved at different points in the story. Help the children to write about an event which involved a race. Did they compete in a race? Did they watch a race? Did anything special happen? As an extension activity you could discuss the behaviour of the characters in this story.

Andrew Brodie: Improving Comprehension for ages 8-9 © A&C Black Publishers Ltd 2008

Sports Day

Name: _____

Date: _____

Answer the questions, using full sentences.

1. Why did Tariq feel that everybody else was better than him?

   _____

   _____

2. In what two ways did Mrs Carson signal the start of the race?

   _____

   _____

3. What did Mrs Carson accuse Tariq of?

   _____

   _____

   _____

4. Do you think she was right? Explain your answer.

   _____

   _____

5. Describe how Tariq won the race.

   _____

   _____

   _____

6. On a separate sheet, write about a sporting event in which you have taken part or have watched.

Notes for teachers
Help the children to read this passage slowly and carefully, discussing the techniques the author uses to build up tension. As an extension activity you could discuss the behaviour of the characters in this story. Did the boys behave well? Did Mrs Carson behave well? Did Tariq behave well? What would they have done in his situation?

Andrew Brodie: Improving Comprehension for ages 8-9 © A&C Black Publishers Ltd 2008

Tirok searches a mystery room

This text is from 'Tirok', a story set in the future, about a boy and his alien friends on a journey to earth. At this point in the story they are just about to uncover a mystery. They have discovered a tunnel on their spaceship that is not shown on any plans.

Inside the tunnel it seemed just like any other but intuitively the three young explorers felt they should walk quietly and not talk at all.

About fifty metres along the tunnel, on the right hand side, they saw a glimmer of light. It came from a barely open door. Ella, who had been leading, silently peered through the narrow chink into the room beyond. Pushing the door open very slowly, she indicated to the others that the room was empty.

In they crept, hearts pounding, knowing they shouldn't be there but too curious not to explore further. The room was full of complex scientific equipment. Tirok felt uneasy. There was something different about this place, something he couldn't quite put his finger on but definitely something odd. It was only much later, back on earth, when thinking about his adventure aboard the 'Endeavour' it occurred to him that the walls hadn't shimmered in the same way as all the others on the ship. At the time however, it was an instinctive uneasiness that helped alert him to the possible danger.

For a short while they gazed in silent amazement at all that surrounded them in the room. Surely it was equipment that should have been in the scientific research area of the vessel, not here amongst the shops, cafes, cinemas and museums?

The silence was broken by the sound of footsteps heading towards the room they were in. All three knew it was time to find a place to hide – and quickly!

Andrew Brodie: Improving Comprehension for ages 8-9 © A&C Black Publishers Ltd 2008

Tirok searches a mystery room

Name: _____

Date: _____

Ring the correct answers to the questions.

1. What is the name of the spacecraft on which they are travelling?

    Endeavour   Enterprise   Elite   Estrange

2. When is the story said to have taken place?

    long ago   recently   in the present   in the future

3. How many young people are in the story?

    one   two   three   four

Answer each of the next questions with a full sentence. The first one has been started for you.

4. What did they find in the room?

    The room was full of _____

5. How was the room different from the other rooms on the spaceship?

    _____

    _____

6. Name two of the characters in the story.

    _____

    _____

7. What did they hear that made them want to hide?

    _____

    _____

Notes for teachers

Before beginning to answer the questions on this page, ensure children understand the text and discuss any unfamiliar words. When tackling the first three questions encourage pupils to look at all the possible answers before deciding which one is correct.

Andrew Brodie: Improving Comprehension for ages 8-9 © A&C Black Publishers Ltd 2008

Tirok searches a mystery room

Name: _____

Date: _____

Ring the correct answers to the questions.

1. Which word is nearest in meaning to 'complex'?

    expensive   complicated   unhappy   large

2. The space ship on which Tirok is travelling is called Endeavour. Which of the words below is nearest in meaning to Endeavour?

    journey   effort   flight   happiness

Answer the questions below using full sentences.

3. Who led the way along the passage?

    _____

    _____

4. Explain why the three friends' hearts were pounding when they first entered the room.

    _____

    _____

5. What broke the silence in the room?

    _____

    _____

6. What did the walls of the passage in the tunnel not do that all the other walls did?

    _____

    _____

Notes for teachers

Ask the children to read the story out loud – they could take it in turns to read. Discuss what is happening in the story and how the characters are feeling at various points. When answering the questions remind pupils of the importance of writing clear sentences with correct punctuation. Encourage pupils to use a dictionary to check the meaning of any unfamiliar words.

Andrew Brodie: Improving Comprehension for ages 8-9 © A&C Black Publishers Ltd 2008

Tirok searches a mystery room

Name: _____

Date: _____

Ring the correct answers to the questions.

1. Which word is nearest in meaning to 'research'?

   games   lessons   study   laugh

2. Which word is nearest in meaning to 'intuitively'?

   instinctively   instructions   reasonably   foolishly

Use complete sentences to answer the following questions.

3. How do you know that Tirok survived this adventure?

   _____

   _____

4. Explain the meaning of the phrase, 'something he couldn't quite put his finger on'.

   _____

   _____

   _____

5. Find two phrases from the text that tell you that the children made no noise when they entered the room.

   _____

   _____

   _____

6. In the final paragraph of the text how does the author convey the possibility of immediate danger?

   _____

   _____

Notes for teachers

The words children have been asked to define on this page are quite complex ones so it would be helpful to discuss the more advanced vocabulary in context before this page is tackled.

Andrew Brodie: Improving Comprehension for ages 8-9 © A&C Black Publishers Ltd 2008

Crossing the road

This extract is from the beginning of 'The Hodgeheg', a story by the author Dick King-Smith.

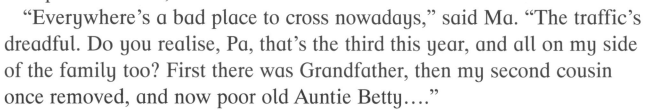

"Your Auntie Betty has copped it," said Pa Hedgehog to Ma.

"Oh no!" cried Ma. "Where?"

"Just down the road. Opposite the newsagent's. Bad place to cross, that."

"Everywhere's a bad place to cross nowadays," said Ma. "The traffic's dreadful. Do you realise, Pa, that's the third this year, and all on my side of the family too? First there was Grandfather, then my second cousin once removed, and now poor old Auntie Betty…."

They were sitting in a flower-bed at their home, the garden of Number 5A of a row of semi-detached houses in a suburban street. On the other side of the road was a Park, very popular with local hedgehogs on account of the good hunting it offered. As well as worms and slugs and

snails, which they could find in their own gardens, there were special attractions in the Park. Mice lived under the Bandstand, feasting on the crumbs dropped from the listeners' sandwiches; frogs dwelt in the Lily-Pond, and in the Ornamental Gardens grass-snakes slithered through the shrubbery. All

these creatures were regarded as great delicacies by the hedgehogs, and they could never resist the occasional night's sport in the Park. But to reach it they had to cross the busy road.

"Poor old Auntie Betty," said Ma again. "It's a hard life and that's fact."

"It's a hard death," said Pa sourly "and that's flat too – talk about squashed, the poor old girl was …."

"Ssssshhhhh!' said Ma at the sound of approaching footsteps. "Not in front of the children," as up trotted four small figures, exact miniatures of their parents except that their spines were still greyish rather than brown.

Andrew Brodie: Improving Comprehension for ages 8-9 © A&C Black Publishers Ltd 2008

Name: _____

Date: _____

Ring the correct answers to the questions.

1. What is the book called?

    The Hedgehog   The Hodgeheg

    The Hedgerow   The Shrubbery

2. Who is the first character to speak?

    Ma   Pa   Auntie Betty   The newsagent

3. Where did the mice live?

    In the   Across the   Under the   In the
    garden   road   bandstand   lily pond

Answer each of the next questions with a full sentence. The first one has been started for you.

4. Who wrote the story?

    The story was _____

5. What was on the other side of the road?

    _____

    _____

6. Where were Ma and Pa sitting?

    _____

    _____

Notes for teachers
Read the passage with the children helping them to tackle any unfamiliar words using their phonic skills. Can they understand the humour in the dialogue between Pa and Ma Hedgehog?

Crossing the road

Name: _____

Date: _____

Ring the correct answer to the question.

1. Which words are nearest in meaning to 'miniatures'?

    huge copies   tiny copies   green copies   blue copies

Answer the next questions with complete sentences.

2. What had happened to Auntie Betty?

    _____

    _____

3. Which creatures lived in the shrubbery?

    _____

    _____

4. Why was the park very popular with the local hedgehogs?

    _____

    _____

5. What made going to the park dangerous?

    _____

    _____

6. How many hedgehogs had died during that year?

    _____

    _____

    _____

Notes for teachers
Read the passage with the children discussing how the author attracts the reader's attention at the beginning through conversation before providing background details in the middle paragraph. Before answering the questions remind pupils of the importance of writing correctly punctuated sentences.

Crossing the road

Name: _____

Date: _____

1. Ring the word or words nearest in meaning to 'delicacies'.

special to eat   easy to break   fun to chase

2. What does Pa mean by 'copped it'?

_____

_____

3. Where did Ma, Pa and the family live?

_____

_____

4. When referring to the mice and what they eat, why do you think the author uses the word 'feasting'?

_____

_____

5. What could the hedgehogs find in both the park and their own garden?

_____

_____

6. Why did Ma say 'not in front of the children'?

_____

_____

_____

_____

_____

Notes for teachers
Ask the children to read the story out loud – they could take it in turns to read. Discuss how the author attracts the reader's attention at the beginning through conversation before providing background details in the middle paragraph. Before answering the questions remind pupils of the importance of writing correctly punctuated sentences.

Andrew Brodie: Improving Comprehension for ages 8-9 © A&C Black Publishers Ltd 2008

The human skeleton

The framework of bones in the human body is called the skeleton. The bones provide support for the whole body and they also give protection for important organs such as the brain, heart and lungs. The bones in our arms and legs operate with our muscles so that we can move about.

The main bones in the head are joined together to form the skull. The skull is connected to the backbone, which itself is made up of smaller bones. Each of these bones in the back is called a vertebra. The plural of vertebra is vertebrae. If you move your hand up and down the centre of your back you can feel a column of lumps. These are the vertebrae.

The ribs are long curved bones that are joined on to the vertebrae in the upper part of the body. They form the framework of the chest, making a protective cage around the heart and lungs.

The bone that forms the upper part of the arm is called the humerus. The two bones of the lower arm, the radius and the ulna, meet the humerus at the elbow and are joined to the hand at the wrist. The hand and fingers have lots of bones.

The upper part of each leg also has only one bone, called the femur. The lower part of the leg has two bones, the tibia and fibula, which meet the femur at the knee. (Look at the diagram – the tibia is the bigger of the two bones.) The bone at the front of the knee is called the patella but it is commonly referred to as the kneecap. The tibia and fibula are joined to the foot at the ankle. Like the hand, the foot has lots of bones.

Andrew Brodie: Improving Comprehension for ages 8-9 © A&C Black Publishers Ltd 2008

The human skeleton

Name: _____

Date: _____

Label the skeleton using the words provided in the word bank.

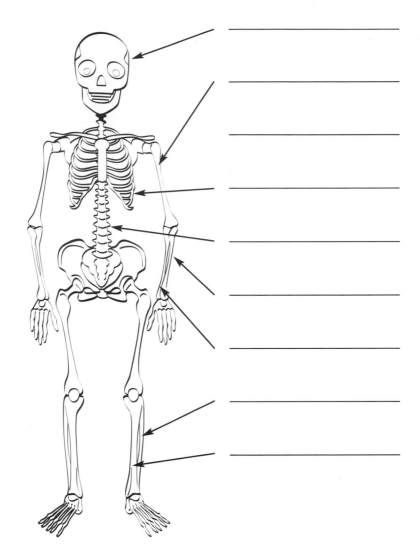

_____

_____

_____

_____

_____

_____

_____

_____

Word bank

skull	vertebrae
ribs	humerus
radius	ulna
femur	tibia
fibula	patella

Why do you think we have a skeleton?

_____

_____

_____

_____

Notes for teachers
Help the children to read the passage slowly and carefully, discussing each part of the skeleton in relation to their own bodies. Ensure that the children understand the task on this sheet then help them to search the text for the clues that they need to label the diagram.

The human skeleton

Name: _____

Date: _____

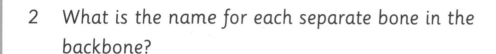

Answer the questions about the skeleton. Write a full sentence for each of your answers.

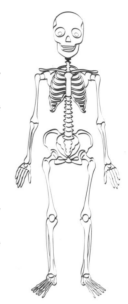

1. Describe one of the main functions of the skeleton.

   _____

   _____

2. What is the name for each separate bone in the backbone?

   _____

   _____

3. What bone forms the upper part of the arm?

   _____

   _____

4. What is the medical name for the kneecap?

   _____

   _____

5. Which two bones are situated between the knee and the ankle?

   _____

   _____

6. Can you think of a creature that does not have a skeleton? What creature is it?

   _____

   _____

Notes for teachers
Help the children to read the passage slowly and carefully, discussing each part of the skeleton in relation to their own bodies. Time permitting you may like the children to complete the 'cat' worksheet before they attempt this one. Ensure the children understand the questions on this sheet. They may need to discuss the word 'functions' for example. The final question may need research in the library or on the computer. The children may suggest animals such as slugs or jellyfish.

Andrew Brodie: Improving Comprehension for ages 8-9 © A&C Black Publishers Ltd 2008

The human skeleton

Name: _____

Date: _____

Answer the questions about the skeleton using full sentences.

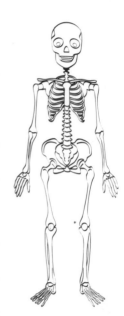

1. What is the singular for 'vertebrae'?

_____

2. Which vital organ does the skull protect?

_____

_____

3. Give the names and positions of the three bones that make up the arm.

_____

_____

_____

_____

4. Which vital organs do the ribs protect?

_____

_____

5. Find some information about the hand to enable you to name some of the bones from which it is formed.

_____

_____

6. Can you think of a creature that does not have a skeleton? Why does it not need a skeleton?

_____

_____

Notes for teachers
Discuss the text with the children, looking at the diagram together and helping them to relate it to their own bodies. The final two questions may need research in the library or on the computer.

A Visit From St. Nicholas by Clement Clarke Moore (Part 1)

'Twas the night before Christmas, when all through the house
Not a creature was stirring, not even a mouse;
The stockings were hung by the chimney with care,
In hopes that St. Nicholas soon would be there.

The children were nestled all snug in their beds,
While visions of sugar-plums danced in their heads;
And mamma in her 'kerchief, and I in my cap,
Had just settled our brains for a long winter's nap.

When out on the lawn there arose such a clatter,
I sprang from my bed to see what was the matter,
Away to the window I flew like a flash,
Tore open the shutters, and threw up the sash.

The moon on the breast of the new fallen snow,
Gave the lustre of midday to objects below;
When, what to my wondering eyes should appear,
But a miniature sleigh and eight tiny reindeer.

With a little old driver so lively and quick,
I knew in a moment it must be St. Nick.
More rapid than eagles his coursers they came,
And he whistled and shouted, and called them by name:

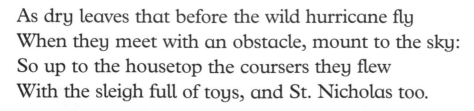

"Now, Dasher! Now, Dancer!
Now, Prancer and Vixen!
On, Comet! On, Cupid!
On, Donner and Blitzen!
To the top of the porch!
To the top of the wall!
Now dash away! Dash away!
Dash away all!"

As dry leaves that before the wild hurricane fly
When they meet with an obstacle, mount to the sky:
So up to the housetop the coursers they flew
With the sleigh full of toys, and St. Nicholas too.

Andrew Brodie: Improving Comprehension for ages 8-9 © A&C Black Publishers Ltd 2008

A Visit From St. Nicholas (Part 1)

Name: _____

Date: _____

Ring the correct answers to the questions.

1. The poem is called A visit from...

   Santa Claus   Father Christmas   St. Nicholas   A reindeer

2. What was the sleigh being pulled by?

   horses   cowsmice   reindeer

3. Which word in the poem is used to rhyme with 'flash'?

   sash   dash   clash   rash

Answer each of the questions with a full sentence. The first one has been started for you.

4. Where were the stockings?

   The stockings were _____

   _____

   _____

5. Where did the sleigh fly up to?

   _____

   _____

6. Who wrote this poem?

   _____

   _____

Notes for teachers
Read the poem through to the children ensuring that they understand that St. Nicholas, St. Nick, Santa Claus and Father Christmas are all names for the same character. Before answering the third question, encourage pupils to look at the way the poem is written in rhyming couplets.

A Visit From St. Nicholas (Part 1)

Name: _____

Date: _____

Ring the correct answers to the questions.

1. Which word is nearest in meaning to 'snug'?

   cold   cosy   careful   climbing

2. Which word is nearest in meaning to 'rapid'?

   quickly   slowly   happily   sadly

3. Choose from the lines below to label the pictures. Be careful! There will be one label left over.

> So up to the housetops the coursers they flew
>
> While visions of sugar-plums danced in their heads.
>
> Tore open the shutters and threw up the sash
>
> Mama in her kerchief and I in my cap

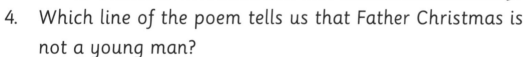

4. Which line of the poem tells us that Father Christmas is not a young man?

   _____

   _____

5. What two words would we usually use for the day or night before Christmas?

   _____

   _____

Notes for teachers
Read the poem with the children ensuring that they understand that St. Nicholas, St. Nick, Santa Claus and Father Christmas are all names for the same character. Discuss any unfamiliar words encouraging children to use their phonic skills to decode them.

Andrew Brodie: Improving Comprehension for ages 8-9 © A&C Black Publishers Ltd 2008

A Visit From St. Nicholas (Part 1)

Name: _____

Date: _____

Ring the correct answers to the questions.

1. Which word is nearest in meaning to 'hurricane'?

    snow   blizzard   rain   wind

2. Which word used in the poem is nearest in meaning to 'stirring'?

    mixing   moving   happy   sad

Answer the questions below using full sentences.

3. Explain what is meant by 'dash away'.

    _____

    _____

4. How many reindeer were there?

    _____

    _____

    _____

5. What is meant in the poem by the words 'wondering eyes'?

    _____

    _____

6. The poem is about St Nicholas. What three other names are used for this character in the poem?

    _____

    _____

    _____

Notes for teachers

Read the poem through with the children ensuring that they understand that St. Nicholas, St. Nick, Santa Claus and Father Christmas are all names for the same character. Help them with the explanation of the phrases in questions 3 and 5, encouraging them to discuss their ideas before writing anything down.

24

A Visit From St. Nicholas by Clement Clarke Moore (Part 2)

And then, in a twinkling, I heard on the roof
The prancing and pawing of each little hoof –
As I drew in my head, and was turning around,
Down the chimney St. Nicholas came with a bound.

He was dressed all in fur, from his head to his foot,
And his clothes were all tarnished with ashes and soot;
A bundle of toys he had flung on his back,
And he looked like a pedlar just opening his pack.

His eyes – how they twinkled; his dimples, how merry!
His cheeks were like roses, his nose like a cherry!
His droll little mouth was drawn up like a bow,
And the beard of his chin was as white as the snow;
The stump of a pipe he held tight in his teeth,
And the smoke it encircled his head like a wreath;
He had a broad face and a little round belly
That shook when he laughed like a bowl full of jelly.

He was chubby and plump, a right jolly old elf,
And I laughed when I saw him, in spite of myself;
A wink of his eye and a twist of his head
Soon gave me to know I had nothing to dread.

He spoke not a word, but went straight to his work,
And he filled all the stockings; then turned with a jerk,
And laying his finger aside of his nose,
And giving a nod, up the chimney he rose.

He sprang to his sleigh, to his team gave a whistle,
And away they all flew like the down of a thistle.
But I heard him exclaim, ere he drove out of sight,
"Happy Christmas to all, and to all a good night!"

25

A Visit From St. Nicholas (Part 2)

Name: _____

Date: _____

Ring the correct answers to the questions.

1. In what was St. Nicholas dressed?

    fur   cotton   wool   nylon

2. What was on his back?

    a reindeer   a carrier bag   a bundle of toys   a rucksack

3. St. Nicholas got in and out of the house through the...

    door   window   roof   chimney

Answer each of the next questions using a full sentence. The first one has been started for you.

4. What colour is his beard?

    His beard _____.

5. What happened when St Nicholas laughed?

    _____

    _____

6. What did his nose look like?

    _____

    _____

7. What did he say as he drove out of sight?

    _____

    _____

Notes for teachers
Remind the children that this is the second part of 'A Visit from St Nicholas' poem. Do they remember what happened in the first part? Help them to read the poem, using their phonic skills to decode any unfamiliar words

26

A Visit From St. Nicholas (Part 2)

Name: _____

Date: _____

Ring the correct answers to the questions.

1. Which word is nearest in meaning to 'hoof'?

   finger   foot   face   fence

2. Which word is nearest in meaning to 'tarnished'?

   stained   covered   dressed   washed

3. Beside each of the following words write the word that it rhymes with in the poem.

   soot   _____   teeth   _____

   jelly   _____   jerk   _____

   snow   _____   thistle   _____

Answer the following questions using complete sentences.

4. What sort of character is St. Nicholas said to be in the poem?

   _____

   _____

5. How did St Nicholas give a signal to tell the reindeer he was ready to leave?

   _____

   _____

6. Who spoke the last words in the poem and what was said?

   _____

   _____

   _____

Notes for teachers
Remind the children that this is the second part of 'A Visit from St Nicholas' poem. Do they remember what happened in the first part? If pupils are unsure of the meaning of 'tarnished' encourage them to check the meaning in a dictionary before returning to the poem.

Andrew Brodie: Improving Comprehension for ages 8-9 © A&C Black Publishers Ltd 2008

A Visit From St. Nicholas (Part 2)

Name: _____

Date: _____

1. Put a ring round the word nearest in meaning to the word 'dread'.

    enjoy   fear   do   unwrap

2. Use a dictionary to help you write a definition for each of the following words. The meaning you give must be the meaning used in the poem.

    droll   _____

    _____

    _____

    stump   _____

    _____

    _____

    bound   _____

    _____

    _____

3. What are the reindeers' hooves described as doing on the roof?

    _____

    _____

4. What was St. Nicholas wearing?

    _____

5. What did St. Nicholas say when doing his work?

    _____

    _____

6. On a separate piece of paper write a description of St. Nicholas

Notes for teachers
Read the poem and the questions through with the children helping them to understand what they need to do. When writing word definitions it is important that pupils write each definition in a way that makes sense in the context of the poem e.g. the word 'bound' must not mean 'to tie up', but rather 'to jump' or 'leap'.

Andrew Brodie: Improving Comprehension for ages 8-9 © A&C Black Publishers Ltd 2008

Winter coughs and colds

Other people cough and sneeze
Look so weary breathing, wheeze.
Sometimes, friends, at home must stay,
Missing school throughout the day.
Voices odd, sound rather hoarse.
Only them, not me of course.
Not me! I'm always very healthy
I NEVER catch a cold!

On cold and frosty winter's days,
Huddled in coats, pale and dismayed.
Throats feel sore, it's hard to swallow
Sneezes soon are sure to follow.
With aches and pains, they call it flu.
Take to their beds; have sips of stew.
Not me! I'm always very healthy
I NEVER catch a cold!

One day last week things seemed to change.
I woke up feeling somewhat strange.
My throat felt odd, and kind of itchy.
My joints hurt and my nose felt twitchy.
My head began to ache and pound.
Got out of bed; the world spun round.
Oh dear I don't feel very healthy.
TODAY I'VE CAUGHT A COLD!

PS.
I feel annoyed about this cold
I caught from someone; young or old.
They coughed, or sneezed without a care.
Spreading their illness everywhere.
Keep your germs so they don't spread
And force other folks to stay in bed.
Then, oh then, we'll ALL stay healthy
And NEVER EVER catch a cold!

Andrew Brodie: Improving Comprehension for ages 8-9 © A&C Black Publishers Ltd 2008

Winter coughs and colds

Name: _____

Date: _____

Put a ring round the correct answer for each question.

1. When you have a cold your voice might sound…

    horse   hoarse   hose   house

2. In the poem, what felt twitchy?

    throat   ears   joints   nose

3. In which season is the poem set?

    Spring   Summer   Autumn   Winter

Answer each of the following questions with a full sentence. The first one has been started for you.

4. What is the poem called?

    The poem is called _____

5. How many verses does the poem have?

    _____

    _____

6. What happened to the poet in the third verse?

    _____

    _____

    _____

7. What are you told to do, in the final verse?

    _____

    _____

    _____

Notes for teachers

Before beginning to answer the questions on this page, ensure children understand the poem. Pay particular attention to any unfamiliar vocabulary. An extension activity suitable for all children would be to design a poster to show how to prevent the spread of coughs and colds.

30

Winter coughs and colds

Name: _____

Date: _____

Put a ring round the correct answer for each question.

1. Which of the words below is nearest in meaning to 'sip'?

    gulp   swallow   big bite   small mouthful

2. Which of the words below is nearest in meaning to 'healthy'?

    ill   well   happy   cold

3. By each of the words below write the rhyming word from the poem.

    swallow _____   course _____

    tissue _____   spread _____

    sneeze _____

Answer the following questions using complete sentences.

4. What do you think the poem is asking you to think about?

    _____

    _____

5. Which illness in the poem causes aches and pains?

    _____

    _____

6. Explain how you know the text is a poem.

    _____

    _____

7. What are we told might follow a sore throat?

    _____

    _____

Notes for teachers

Read the poem together and discuss how children know it's a poem i.e. the layout, the verses and the rhyming element of the text. An extension activity suitable for all children would be to design a poster to show how to prevent the spread of coughs and colds.

31

Andrew Brodie: Improving Comprehension for ages 8-9 © A&C Black Publishers Ltd 2008

Winter coughs and colds

Name: _____

Date: _____

Answer the questions with using full sentences.

1. Explain what is meant by a voice sounding 'hoarse'.

    _____

    _____

2. Explain what is meant by 'huddled'.

    _____

    _____

3. Why have some words in the poem been written in capital letters?

    _____

    _____

4. How did the writer think she had caught a cold?

    _____

    _____

5. Give two reasons why people might look pale in the winter.

    _____

    _____

6. Explain what is meant in the poem by 'Got out of bed; the world spun round.'

    _____

    _____

7. What does P.S. stand for?

    _____

    _____

Andrew Brodie: Improving Comprehension for ages 8-9 © A&C Black Publishers Ltd 2008

Air-raid

Mary sat up in bed rubbing her eyes.

"Come on love," said Mum. "Hurry up, the siren went off five minutes ago."

Mary forced herself out of bed, put her feet into her slippers and pulled on her dressing gown. She sighed as she tied the cord around her waist. This happened every night and every night there seemed to be no reason. True, she had heard aeroplanes passing high overhead but there had been no bombs, no explosions, no sounds of emergency bells … at least, not in her street.

Reluctantly she plodded down the stairs and turned towards the kitchen.

"Hurry up, Mary!" said Mum crossly as she opened the door to the under-stairs cupboard.

"Do we have to go in here again?" asked Mary, just as crossly. "Nothing ever happens."

"Yes but it might," said Mum.

"I wish Dad was here," said Mary.

"So do I love," said Mum, "but, he'll be home in a few weeks."

Mary felt a bit happier and settled down on the pile of cushions that they'd put in the cupboard to make it more comfortable. Mum lit the candle and Mary picked up a pencil to write on the wood on the underside of the stairs.

"What rhymes with dog?" she asked.

"Frog … log … slog … fog," suggested Mum.

Mary began to write a poem, pressing hard with the pencil on one wooden stair.

Once there was a dog,

Who got lost in the fog.

When he got home to bed,

He slept like a …

BANG.

The explosion must have been very close … maybe even in their street, … maybe even in their house.

Mary clutched on to her mum and was surprised to find her mum shaking.

"It'll be all right, Mum," she said.

Andrew Brodie: Improving Comprehension for ages 8-9 © A&C Black Publishers Ltd 2008

Air-raid

Name: _____

Date: _____

Answer the questions using full sentences. Check your punctuation carefully.

1. What is the name of the girl in the story?

   _____

   _____

2. Why did she have to get up during the night?

   _____

   _____

3. Where did she have to go?

   _____

   _____

4. How had they made their cupboard more comfortable?

   _____

   _____

5. How did Mary spend the time?

   _____

   _____

6. Write out Mary's poem, filling in the missing word.

   _____

   _____

   _____

   _____

Notes for teachers

Help the children to read the passage slowly and carefully, ensuring that they understand that the story is set a very long time ago during World War Two and that the story ends with a bomb dropping near Mary's house. Discuss the fact that for some children, sleeping in an air-raid shelter was a nightly ritual during part of World War Two. The pupils might also be aware that some children were evacuated to the country from the cities to spare them the dangers of the air-raids. Ask the children to say their answers out loud before they write anything down as this can help with sentence structure and punctuation.

Andrew Brodie: Improving Comprehension for ages 8-9 © A&C Black Publishers Ltd 2008

Name: _____

Date: _____

Answer the questions, using full sentences.

1. How did Mary's mum know that they had to go to the shelter?

    _____

    _____

2. Why was Mum cross?

    _____

    _____

3. Why was Mary cross?

    _____

    _____

4. Why did Mary ask what rhymes with 'dog'?

    _____

    _____

5. What caused the bang?

    _____

    _____

6. Have you had a strange experience at night? Write about it.

    _____

    _____

    _____

    _____

    _____

Andrew Brodie: Improving Comprehension for ages 8-9 © A&C Black Publishers Ltd 2008

Name: _____

Date: _____

Answer the questions, using full sentences. Check your punctuation carefully.

1. How did Mary feel about getting up in the middle of the night?

    _____

    _____

2. Why did she feel that it was a waste of time sheltering under the stairs?

    _____

    _____

3. Why did Mum insist that they went into their shelter?

    _____

    _____

4. Why do you think Mary's dad is not at home?

    _____

    _____

5. At the end of the story, why was Mary's mum shaking?

    _____

    _____

6. Mary had to spend time in a cupboard. On a separate piece of paper write about a time when you were in a strange or unusual place.

Notes for teachers

Help the children to read the passage slowly and carefully, ensuring that they understand that the story is set during World War Two. Discuss the fact that for some children sleeping in an air-raid shelter was a nightly ritual during part of World War Two. The pupils might also be aware that some children were evacuated to the country from the cities to spare them from the dangers of the air-raids. Pupils might need some help coming up with and deciding on an experience for the final question. Encourage them to include indications of how they felt in the strange place.

Andrew Brodie: Improving Comprehension for ages 8-9 © A&C Black Publishers Ltd 2008

Daily Gazette

DAILY NEWSPAPER

Rescue of the Innocents

We are pleased to report that one and a half million children and mothers with babies have been successfully evacuated to places of safety. Tearful parents have delivered their offspring to railway stations from where the brave youngsters have travelled to their new homes in the country.

The evacuees set off into the unknown, bearing labels fastened to their coats and carrying spare clothes in bags or small suitcases. Their parents remain in the cities facing the dangers of air-raids from the Luftwaffe, Hitler's mighty air-force.

For many children the arrival in the countryside has been a novelty. Their billets may be isolated farmhouses or cottages, quite unlike their homes in the cities. Peaceful villages and muddy farms are new experiences and meeting a flock of sheep or a herd of cows in a country lane can be a real eye-opener for those used to the busy streets of London or Manchester.

The experience of welcoming the evacuees on the country railway stations has proved to be a shock for country folk not familiar with city accents. In some homes country children find themselves sharing their bedrooms with children from the city, hopefully making new friendships in these difficult times.

For the billeters, the arrival of the young guests provides a useful addition to their weekly income. They are paid ten shillings and sixpence for one child. If they provide a home for more than one child they are paid an extra eight shillings and sixpence for each additional evacuee.

Let us all hope that the evacuation will be short-lived and that the young people will be able to return to their homes and families in the not too distant future.

Andrew Brodie: Improving Comprehension for ages 8-9 © A&C Black Publishers Ltd 2008

Rescue of the Innocents

Name: _____

Date: _____

Read the newspaper article carefully. You may need to read it several times. Answer the questions using full sentences.

1. What is the name of the newspaper in which the article appears?

   _____

   _____

2. Why did the children travel to the country?

   _____

   _____

3. How did they get there?

   _____

   _____

4. What might the evacuees meet on a country lane?

   _____

   _____

5. What special name is used for the host families?

   _____

   _____

6. Write about how you might feel if you were sent away from your home and family.

   _____

   _____

   _____

Notes for teachers
Read the passage through with the children helping them to understand the content of the newspaper report. They need to be aware that the style is typical of a newspaper report written during the Second World War. A billet is the term for a place where troops are lodged with civilians, but in the Second World War it was also used to describe to where children were evacuated. Discuss the report with them to ensure that they understand that children have been sent to the country, away from the dangers of the air-raids. Point out that some children still stayed in towns and cities where air-raids took place.

38

Andrew Brodie: Improving Comprehension for ages 8-9 © A&C Black Publishers Ltd 2008

Rescue of the Innocents

Name: _____

Date: _____

Answer the questions, using full sentences.

1. Who were evacuated to the country?

   _____

   _____

2. Why were they evacuated?

   _____

   _____

3. What did the evacuees take with them?

   _____

   _____

4. What special name is used to describe the homes where the evacuees are staying?

   _____

   _____

5. What advantage do the billeters gain from having the evacuees to stay?

   _____

   _____

6. Imagine that you are a country child during the Second World War. On a separate piece of paper describe how you feel having an evacuee to stay with you.

Notes for teachers
Read the passage through to the children helping them to understand the story. They need to be aware that the style is typical of a newspaper report written during the Second World War. Discuss the story with them to ensure that they understand that children have been sent to the country, away from the dangers of the air-raids. Point out that some children still stayed in towns and cities where air-raids took place. Read the questions with the children ensuring that they understand them, particularly the word 'billeters' in question 5. See Notes for teachers on p38.

Rescue of the Innocents

Name: _____

Date: _____

Answer the questions, using full sentences. Check your punctuation carefully.

1. Several words have been used in place of the word 'children'. Find three examples and explain why each one has been used.

    _____

    _____

    _____

2. What might the billeters find difficult about providing a home for the evacuees?

    _____

    _____

3. One shilling is equivalent to five new pence. 'Sixpence' is equivalent to two and a half new pence. What were the billeters paid for hosting one evacuee? Give your answer in shillings and pence and in modern money.

    _____

    _____

4. Imagine that you are the mother of a child who is sent to the country. Describe how you feel.

    _____

    _____

    _____

    _____

    _____

Notes for teachers
Discuss the report with the pupils ensuring that they understand that the evacuee children have been sent to the country, away from the dangers of the air-raids. Point out that some children still stayed in towns and cities where air-raids took place. Discuss the children's ideas and thoughts for question 4 before they write anything down. See Notes for teachers on p38 for a definition of 'billet'.

The Competition

This extract is from Horrid Henry's Stinkbomb by Francesca Simon.

Blah blah blah blah blah.

Miss Battle-Axe droned on and on and on. Horrid Henry drew pictures of crocodiles tucking into a juicy Battle-Axe snack in his maths book.

Snap! Off went her head.

Yank! Bye bye leg.

Crunch! Ta-ta teeth.

Yum yum. Henry's crocodile had a big fat smile on its face.

Blah blah blah books blah blah blah read blah blah blah prize blah blah

… PRIZE?

Horrid Henry stopped doodling.

"What prize?" he shrieked.

"Don't shout out, Henry," said Miss Battle-Axe.

Horrid Henry waved his hand and shouted:

"What prize?"

"Well, Henry, if you'd been paying attention instead of scribbling, you'd know, wouldn't you?" said Miss Battle-Axe.

Horrid Henry scowled. Typical teacher. You're interested enough in what they're saying to ask a question, and suddenly they don't want to answer.

"So class, as I was saying before I was so rudely interrupted- " she glared at Horrid Henry- "you'll have two weeks to read as many books as you can for our school reading competition. Whoever reads the most books will win an exciting prize. A very exciting prize. But remember, a book report on every book on your list, please."

Oh. A reading competition. Horrid Henry slumped in his chair. Phooey. Reading was hard, heavy work. Just turning the pages made Henry feel exhausted. Why couldn't they ever do fun competitions, like whose tummy could rumble the loudest, or who shouted out most in class, or who knew the rudest words? Horrid Henry could win those competitions every time.

Andrew Brodie: Improving Comprehension for ages 8-9 © A&C Black Publishers Ltd 2008

The Competition

Name: _____

Date: _____

Answer the questions, using full sentences.

1. From which book does the passage come?

   _____

   _____

2. Who wrote the book?

   _____

   _____

3. What does 'Blah blah blah blah blah' mean?

   _____

   _____

4. Why did Horrid Henry shout out?

   _____

   _____

5. How could the children win a prize?

   _____

   _____

6. Why did Horrid Henry slump in his chair?

   _____

   _____

7. Give an example of the type of competition that Horrid Henry thinks he could win.

   _____

   _____

Notes for teachers
Read the passage through with the children helping them to understand the story and to decode any unfamiliar words. Help them to compose sentences to answer the questions, encouraging them to say the sentences out loud before writing anything down.

Andrew Brodie: Improving Comprehension for ages 8-9 © A&C Black Publishers Ltd 2008

The Competition

Name: _____

Date: _____

Answer the questions, using full sentences.

1. Who is the author of the book from which this passage comes?

   _____

   _____

2. Who do you think Miss Battle-Axe is?

   _____

   _____

3. What were the crocodiles doing in Horrid Henry's pictures?

   _____

   _____

4. Why did Horrid Henry stop doodling?

   _____

   _____

5. How long have the children got to read the books?

   _____

   _____

6. What does Horrid Henry think of reading?

   _____

   _____

7. What type of competitions does Horrid Henry want?

   _____

   _____

Notes for teachers
Ask the children to read the story out loud helping them to appreciate the humour in the story. They could take it in turns to read. Help them to compose sentences to answer the questions, encouraging them to say the sentences out loud before writing anything down.

The Competition

Name: _____

Date: _____

Answer the questions, using full sentences. Check your punctuation carefully.

1. What is Miss Battle-Axe doing at the start of the story?

    _____

2. What do you think Horrid Henry thinks of Miss Battle-Axe?

    _____

    _____

3. What do you think Miss Battle-Axe thinks of Horrid Henry?

    _____

    _____

4. What did Horrid Henry call out in class?

    _____

    _____

5. Do you think Miss Battle-Axe was fair to Horrid Henry?

    _____

    _____

6. Do you think Horrid Henry was fair to Miss Battle-Axe?

    _____

    _____

7. What do you think was the most difficult part of the competition?

    _____

    _____

Notes for teachers

Ask the children to read the story out loud. They could take on the parts of Horrid Henry, Miss Battle-Axe and the narrator. Read the questions with the children ensuring that they understand them. With questions 2 and 3 discuss with the children how they know what each character thinks of the other.

Mute Swan

General information

The mute swan is much more common in Britain than the other two species that can be found here, the Whooper swan and the Bewick's swan.

Habitat

The mute swan can be found on lakes, ponds, rivers and canals and sometimes on the sea near the coast.

Identification

The mute swan is a very large white bird with a long neck and an orange bill. The bill has a large black lump called a knob near the bird's eye. The young birds, called cygnets, are grey in colour. Mute swans produce few sounds apart from hissing; their large wings produce a beating or humming sound as they fly.

Food

They mainly eat vegetation in the water but they will also eat grass in fields near water.

Nesting

The male bird collects sticks, reeds and other vegetation and brings them to the female. She then builds a very large nest on the ground or in reed-beds. There are usually between five and seven eggs, which are grey-green in colour and are laid in March, April or May. The parents take turns to incubate the eggs for about five weeks. Both parents look after the cygnets who are able to swim one or two days after hatching. They learn to fly about sixteen weeks later.

Andrew Brodie: Improving Comprehension for ages 8-9 © A&C Black Publishers Ltd 2008

Mute Swan

Name: _____

Date: _____

Look at the information about mute swans, then answer the questions below.

1. In how many sections is the information arranged?

    _____

    _____

2. Which swan builds the nest?

    _____

    _____

3. Which section would tell us where the birds might live?

    _____

    _____

4. What do mute swans eat?

    _____

    _____

5. Which section tells us what the birds look like?

    _____

    _____

6. Write about a bird or an animal, describing what it looks like.

    _____

    _____

    _____

    _____

46

Name: _____

Date: _____

Look at the information about mute swans, then answer the questions below using full sentences.

1. What colour are the young swans?

    _____

    _____

2. What other species of swan can be found in this country?

    _____

    _____

3. What special word means 'sit on' the eggs to keep them warm?

    _____

    _____

4. What sounds do mute swans make?

    _____

    _____

5. Where do mute swans build their nests?

    _____

    _____

6. On a separate sheet of paper, write about an animal or bird using the headings 'Identification' and 'Habitat', and 'Food'. You may need to look in a book or on the Internet to find information.

Notes for teachers
Discuss the text with the pupils and that fact that because it's non-fiction it is designed so that information can be found quickly. For the last task the children could describe a pet at home. Encourage them to think carefully what the pet's habitat is!

Andrew Brodie: Improving Comprehension for ages 8-9 © A&C Black Publishers Ltd 2008

Mute Swan

Name: _____

Date: _____

Look at the information about mute swans, then answer the questions using full sentences. Check your punctuation carefully.

1. How many cygnets do the swans have when they breed?

    _____

    _____

2. How do the adult birds cooperate to build a nest?

    _____

    _____

3. What does the word 'mute' mean? Use a dictionary to find out.

    _____

    _____

    _____

4. Why is this species called the 'mute' swan?

    _____

    _____

5. If a pair of mute swans lay their eggs in early April, in what month
    would the cygnets learn to fly? (Assume that a month is about four
    weeks long.)

    _____

    _____

6. Using books or a computer find out about Whooper swans or Bewick's
    swans. On a separate piece of paper describe how they are different
    from mute swans.

Notes for teachers
Discuss the text with the pupils and that fact that because it's non-fiction it is designed so that information can be found quickly. Help the children to compose answers orally before they attempt to write anything down.

Andrew Brodie: Improving Comprehension for ages 8-9 © A&C Black Publishers Ltd 2008

The Village

Ben was asked to write about the village where he lives as part of his work in geography. His teacher told him that he could find information about the village by looking carefully at a map. Mr Brown also told Ben that he should try to be as accurate as possible when giving distances or descriptions and that he should only write about relevant facts. This is what Ben wrote:

My village is called Sampford Fitzpaine. I live in a cottage in a row of houses called Days Meadow. Days Meadow is about two hundred and fifty metres north-east of my school, Sampford Fitzpaine Primary School.

The church is about one hundred metres north-west of the school. There was a post office about one hundred metres south-east of the school but that closed down last year. I used to buy my sweets there.

The main road through the village goes right past the school but it's not very busy. When we did a survey in maths we found that seventeen vehicles went past in one hour. There were four tractors, two vans, a lorry and ten cars. Mrs Thornton went past on her bike too.

There are two farms in the village. One is called Home Farm and has mainly pigs. The other is Fitzpaine Farm and it has cattle and sheep.

Our school field is not joined to the school. It's the other side of Days Meadow and there is a footpath to get there. The village green is opposite the school and every year the village fete happens there. The cricket field is about a kilometre away, in a south-easterly direction.

The nearest town is called Tavington and it is five kilometres east of Sampford Fitzpaine.

I like my village because everybody is very friendly. I like living in the country because there are lots of animals and there are fields and woods to play in.

Andrew Brodie: Improving Comprehension for ages 8-9 © A&C Black Publishers Ltd 2008

The Village

Name: _____

Date: _____

1. What is the name of Ben's teacher?

    _____

    _____

2. What is Ben's village called?

    _____

    _____

3. How far from the school does Ben live?

    _____

    _____

4. What happens on the village green every year?

    _____

    _____

5. What is the nearest town to Ben's village?

    _____

    _____

6. Write about where you live.

    _____

    _____

    _____

    _____

    _____

Notes for teachers
Help the children to read the passage slowly and carefully, taking the opportunity to practise maths and geography skills by drawing a very simple sketch map to match Ben's description of the relative layout of his village – they can decide for themselves where to place the two farms. They might need to discuss their ideas for question 6 before writing anything down.

50

The Village

Name: _____

Date: _____

1. What did the teacher suggest that Ben should use to find information?

   _____

   _____

2. How else could Ben find out information about the village?

   _____

   _____

3. Where is the church in relation to the school?

   _____

   _____

4. What does Ben miss about the post office?

   _____

   _____

5. What farm animals could you find in the village?

   _____

   _____

6. Write about your school and the buildings near it.

   _____

   _____

   _____

   _____

   _____

   _____

Notes for teachers
Help the children to read the passage slowly and carefully, taking the opportunity to practise maths and geography skills by drawing a very simple sketch map to match Ben's description of the relative layout of his village – they can decide for themselves where to place the two farms.

Andrew Brodie: Improving Comprehension for ages 8-9 © A&C Black Publishers Ltd 2008

1. Explain how one word shows that Mr Brown is Ben's teacher.

   _____

   _____

2. What sort of house does Ben live in?

   _____

   _____

3. What is inconvenient about the school field?

   _____

   _____

   _____

4. List all the places where Ben could play.

   _____

   _____

5. Give an example from the passage where Ben does not write in the style that Mr Brown asked for.

   _____

   _____

6. Write about an area that you know well.

   _____

   _____

   _____

   _____

   _____

Notes for teachers
Help the children to read the passage slowly and carefully, taking the opportunity to practise maths and geography skills by drawing a very simple sketch map to match Ben's description of the relative layout of his village – they can decide for themselves where to place the two farms. Encourage the children to write complete sentences when answering the questions, ensuring that they use appropriate punctuation.

Into the pit

The extract below is from Stig of the Dump by Clive King. It concerns a boy called Barney who goes to see an old chalk pit that is now used as a rubbish tip.

He crawled through the rough grass and peered over. The sides of the pit were white chalk, with lines of flint poking out like bones in places. At the top was crumbly brown earth and the roots of trees that grew on the edge. The roots looped over the edge, twined in the air and grew back into the earth. Some of the trees hung over the edge, holding on desperately by a few roots. The earth and chalk had fallen away beneath them, and one day they too would fall to the bottom of the pit. Strings of ivy and the creeper called Old Man's Beard hung in the air.

Far below was the bottom of the pit. The dump. Barney could see strange bits of wreckage among the moss and elder bushes and nettles. Was that the steering wheel of a ship? The tail of an aeroplane? At least there was a real bicycle. Barney felt sure he could make it go if only he could get at it. They didn't let him have a bicycle.

Barney wished he was at the bottom of the pit.

And the ground gave way.

Barney felt his head going down and his feet going up. There was a rattle of falling earth beneath him. Then he was falling, still clutching the clump of grass that was falling with him.

'This is what it's like when the ground gives way,' thought Barney. Then he seemed to turn a complete somersault in the air, bumped into a ledge of chalk half-way down, crashed through some creepers and ivy and branches, and landed on a bank of moss.

His thoughts did those funny things they do when you bump your head and you suddenly find yourself thinking about what you had for dinner last Tuesday, all mixed up with seven times six. Barney lay with his eyes shut, waiting for his thoughts to stop being mixed up. Then he opened them.

He was lying in a kind of shelter. Looking up he could see a roof, or part of a roof, made of elder branches, a very rotten old carpet, and rusty old sheets of iron. There was a big hole, through which he must have fallen. He could see the white walls of the cliff, the trees and creepers at the top, and the sky with clouds passing over it.

Andrew Brodie: Improving Comprehension for ages 8-9 © A&C Black Publishers Ltd 2008

Into the pit

1. From which book does the passage come?

   _____

   _____

2. Who wrote the book?

   _____

   _____

3. Apart from the trees which two other plants are growing on the edge of the pit?

   _____

   _____

4. How did Barney get to the bottom of the pit?

   _____

   _____

5. Why did Barney have a soft landing?

   _____

   _____

6. How would you have felt if you had fallen in a hole like this?

   _____

   _____

   _____

   _____

   _____

   _____

Notes for teachers
Read the passage through with the children helping them to understand the story and to decode any unfamiliar words. Help them to think up ideas for the final task, encouraging them to consider details about the place they are describing. Look through the passage again, pointing out the details in relation to the sides of the pit, the rubbish that was in the pit, the way Barney fell, etc.

Into the pit

Name: _____

Date: _____

1. Who is the author of the book from which this passage comes?

   _____

   _____

2. What was the pit used for?

   _____

   _____

3. What did Barney think he could see in the pit?

   _____

   _____

4. Why did Barney wish he was at the bottom of the pit?

   _____

   _____

5. Do you think Barney was badly injured?

   _____

   _____

6. Barney wanted to be at the bottom of the pit. Where would you wish to be and why would you like to be there?

   _____

   _____

   _____

   _____

   _____

   _____

   _____

Notes for teachers

Ask the children to read the story out loud – they could take it in turns. Help them to think up ideas for the final task, encouraging them to consider details about the place they are describing. Look through the passage again, pointing out the details in relation to the sides of the pit, the rubbish that was in the pit, the way Barney fell, etc.

Andrew Brodie: Improving Comprehension for ages 8-9 © A&C Black Publishers Ltd 2008

Into the pit

Name: _____

Date: _____

1. Why would some of the trees fall into the pit one day?

   _____

   _____

2. Who do you think wouldn't let Barney have a bicycle?

   _____

   _____

3. Why do you think the ground gave way?

   _____

   _____

4. What did Barney bump into?

   _____

   _____

5. Where was Barney's landing place?

   _____

   _____

6. Write about the most unusual place you have ever been. Describe it using as many details as possible – details make descriptions interesting.

   _____

   _____

   _____

   _____

   _____

   _____

Notes for teachers

Ask the children to take it in turns to read the story out loud. Read the questions with the children ensuring that they understand them. Help them to compose the answers out loud before writing anything down.

Soap

When you wash each day have you ever wondered where and when soap was first used?

On this page find some fascinating facts about soap.

The very first people did not have soap, but they would wash in the water of rivers and streams.

The ancient Egyptians bathed regularly to keep clean. They may have used oils on their skin and then scraped it off, bringing off dirt as well as the perfumed oils.

The use of some type of soap, though probably not soap as we know it today, is mentioned in the Old Testament of the Bible. Do you know where? It would be interesting to look.

The name 'soap' possibly came from a Roman Legend telling of Mount Sapo, where animals were sacrificed. When it rained, a mixture of wood ashes and animal fat ran into the river Tiber. People washing their clothes in this water found their washing easier to do and much cleaner.

Early forms of soap were made from oils mixed with ashes from plants and some perfume to make it smell pleasant.

Bathing went out of fashion in Europe for many hundreds of years and crowded towns and cities must have been very smelly.

Soap making in England began in the 14th century. Soap was considered a luxury item and used only by the wealthy.

It was not until Victorian times that soap became widely used as people became more aware of the importance of keeping clean.

Nowadays we all use soap on a regular basis, either in the form of a bar or as a liquid that we squirt out of a bottle. What would we do without it?

Andrew Brodie: Improving Comprehension for ages 8-9 © A&C Black Publishers Ltd 2008

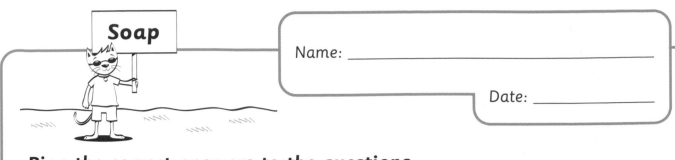

Soap

Name: _____

Date: _____

Ring the correct answers to the questions.

1. Where did people first wash?

    streams   bushes   jacuzzi   swimming
    and rivers   and trees   baths   pools

2. What did the ancient Egyptians put on their skin?

    boils   oils   bananas   ashes

3. When did soap making begin in England?

    14th century   18th century   10th century   15th century

Answer each of the next questions with a full sentence. The first one has been started for you.

4. When did soap become widely used in England?

    Soap became widely _____

    _____

    _____

5. Which mountain is talked about in the Roman legend?

    _____

    _____

6. Why were the towns and cities in Europe very smelly for many hundreds of years?

    _____

    _____

Notes for teachers
Before beginning to answer the questions on this page, ensure children understand the text. Pay particular attention to any unfamiliar vocabulary. Have they learnt anything about the history of soap? What can they tell you about it?

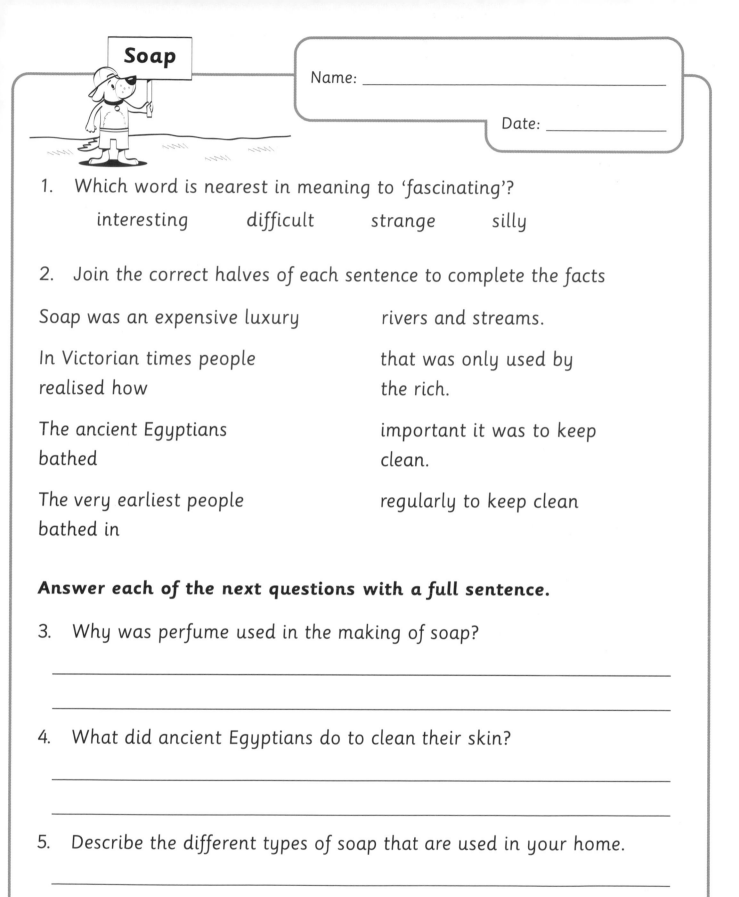

Soap

Name: _____

Date: _____

1. Which word is nearest in meaning to 'fascinating'?

    interesting   difficult   strange   silly

2. Join the correct halves of each sentence to complete the facts

Soap was an expensive luxury   rivers and streams.

In Victorian times people   that was only used by
realised how   the rich.

The ancient Egyptians   important it was to keep
bathed   clean.

The very earliest people   regularly to keep clean
bathed in

Answer each of the next questions with a full sentence.

3. Why was perfume used in the making of soap?

    _____

    _____

4. What did ancient Egyptians do to clean their skin?

    _____

    _____

5. Describe the different types of soap that are used in your home.

    _____

    _____

    _____

Notes for teachers
Before pupils tackle the final task on this page they should discuss different sorts of soap they know about, for
example, tablets to wash clothes, washing up liquid to wash dishes, shampoo to wash hair.

Andrew Brodie: Improving Comprehension for ages 8-9 © A&C Black Publishers Ltd 2008

Soap

Name: _____

Date: _____

1. What do you notice about the name of the mountain in the Roman legend?

   _____

   _____

2. In the legend what are we told happened on the mountain?

   _____

   _____

3. Into which river did the ashes and animal fat go?

   _____

   _____

4. Which of the following ingredients is not mentioned as used to make soap?

   oil   perfume   flour   ashes

5. Write a definition for each of the following words.

   wealthy _____

   _____

   luxury _____

   _____

   fashion _____

   _____

6. On a separate sheet of paper, write about why it is important to use soap.

Notes for teachers
Encourage pupils to use a dictionary when writing their definitions for question 5. An extension activity could be to design a poster explaining the importance of good hygiene.

Andrew Brodie: Improving Comprehension for ages 8-9 © A&C Black Publishers Ltd 2008

Clearing the clutter

The house has been tidied. Now where has everything
been carefully put away?

Let me find my things first.
When Mum does a clean, the toys
won't be seen.
Up in the loft, there are
building blocks
Under the stairs, go the
Teddy bears.
In bedrooms stay, all the
games to play.
Put on the shelf, is the
clockwork elf.
My doll, in the cupboard, is called
Mother Hubbard.

Now where have all Dad's bits and pieces been put?

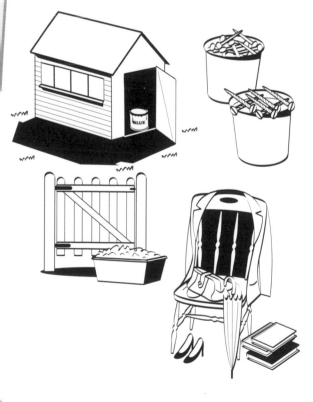

His keys, a bunch, in the box
with his lunch.
In some old pails, go the
screws and nails.
Paints of blue and red, go
in the shed.
Into the garage, go the
tools that are large.
In the hall, by the wall, go the
tools that are small.
Out by the gate, goes rubbish
in a crate.

Where has Mum put away her own
things?
What a surprise, they all seem to be just
where they started.

Andrew Brodie: Improving Comprehension for ages 8-9 © A&C Black Publishers Ltd 2008

Clearing the clutter

Name: _____

Date: _____

Ring the correct answers.

1. The title of the poem is ...

   Cleaning the garage   Tidying the house   Clearing the clutter

2. Up in the loft are..

   toys   teddy bears   building blocks   a doll

3. Where do the paints go?

   In the garage   In the shed   In the loft   By the gate

Answer each of the next questions with a full sentence. The first one has been started for you.

4. Where have the screws and nails been put?

   The screws and nails _____

   _____

   _____

5. Where did the teddy bears go?

   _____

   _____

6. Who has been tidying the house?

   _____

   _____

7. Whose things are still left where they started?

   _____

   _____

Notes for teachers

Before they begin to answer the questions on this page, ensure that the children understand the text. Pay particular attention to any unfamiliar vocabulary.

Andrew Brodie: Improving Comprehension for ages 8-9 © A&C Black Publishers Ltd 2008

Clearing the clutter

Name: _____

Date: _____

Ring the correct answers.

1. Which word is nearest in meaning to 'pails'?

    pots   pans   buckets   bowls

2. What will stay in the bedrooms?

    the elf   the games   the keys   the screws and nails

3. By each of the following items write down the name of the place they have been put.

    small tools _____

    large tools _____

    clockwork elf _____

    bunch of keys _____

    teddy bears _____

Answer the following questions with complete sentences.

4. What is the name of the item that has been put in the cupboard?

    _____

    _____

5. What can be found by the gate?

    _____

    _____

6. Where has Mum put her things?

    _____

    _____

Notes for teachers
Before they begin to answer the questions on this page, ensure that the children understand the text. Pay particular attention to any unfamiliar vocabulary. Remind pupils of the importance of writing clear sentences with correct punctuation.

Clearing the clutter

Name: _____

Date: _____

1. Who has been clearing away the clutter in the house?

   _____

   _____

2. Explain how the two main verses of the poem have been structured?

   _____

   _____

   _____

   _____

3. What is the purpose of the questions in the poem?

   _____

   _____

   _____

   _____

4. How have the tools in the poem been sorted out?

   _____

   _____

5. The poet uses the words 'what a surprise'. Do you think it is really a surprise that Mum's things are still where they started? Explain your answer.

   _____

   _____

   _____

Notes for teachers

Before pupils tackle this page, discuss the way the poem has been structured – this should include the number of lines in each verse, the rhyming features and the way the first rhyme in each pair does not come at the end of the line though when read aloud the rhyme can clearly be heard. Pay particular attention to the words 'what a surprise' ask pupils to read it with expression to lead to an understanding that the way something is said can convey its real meaning. As an extension activity ask pupils to invent a new verse for the poem. They might work on this task in pairs or small groups.

Andrew Brodie: Improving Comprehension for ages 8-9 © A&C Black Publishers Ltd 2008